How do I feel about

BEING JEALOUS

Sarah Levete

COPPER BEECH BOOKS • BROOKFIELD, CONNECTICUT

Designed and produced by
Aladdin Books Ltd
28 Percy Street
London W1P 0LD

First published in the United States
in 1999 by
Copper Beech Books,
an imprint of
The Millbrook Press
2 Old New Milford Road
Brookfield, Connecticut 06804

Printed in Belgium
5 4 3 2 1

Designer   Gary Edgar-Hyde
Editor   Jon Richards
Illustrator   Christopher O'Neill
Photographer   Roger Vlitos

CIP data for this publication is
available in the Library of Congress.

ISBN 0-7613-0911-X (lib. bdg.)

Contents

Introduction

Matt, Prem, Adam, Oona, and Abi go to the same school. Adam, Prem, and Abi have felt jealous of other people or their belongings. Oona and Matt know what it feels like when someone is jealous of them. Have you ever felt jealous? Join the friends as they discuss their feelings.

Being jealous can make you unkind to the people you love.

I was jealous of my brother. It made me feel lonely.

Everyone is different and has different belongings.

It's upsetting if someone is jealous of you.

Jealousy can make you fed up with the things you have.

MATT PREM ADAM OONA ABI

What Is Jealousy?

Adam and Abi always walk to school together. Today, Abi is in a bad mood. She is jealous because her friend, Oona, has got some new clothes. Adam used to be jealous of his brother, Sam. He thought his mom loved Sam more than him. Jealousy is a feeling that what someone else has, or does, is better than what you have, or do.

You may feel jealous for a moment…

I'm really jealous of Oona. She's always got new things.

I used to be jealous of my brother. I thought he was mom's favorite.

… or you may feel jealous for a long time.

▽ *Jealous About Things*

Some people feel jealous of other's belongings. They may worry that what they have will be taken away from them. People who feel this kind of jealousy can find it hard to share their toys and games.

◁ *Jealous About People*

Have you ever felt angry with a person because he or she is good at something? This is feeling jealous about a person. It can make you think that no one takes any notice of you or that you are less special than the other person.

Adam, why were you jealous of your brother, Sam?

"Sam was allowed to do all the things I wasn't allowed to do. Even when he was naughty, nobody ever got angry with him. I never had new clothes. I always used to have his old things."

5

Jealous About Belongings

Abi and Matt are going for a bike ride, but Abi is in a bad mood again. This time it's because her mom won't buy her a new pair of sneakers like Oona's. Matt thinks Abi is being silly — she's already got a great pair of sneakers!

Have you ever wanted something you couldn't have? How did it make you feel?

It's not fair. Mom won't let me have new sneakers like Oona's.

Why do you want new sneakers? What's wrong with yours?

1. Tom was given a computer game for his birthday. He really liked it.

2. Two days later, Tom's friend, Pete, was given a different game.

It's not fair. I wanted a game like Pete's. It's much better than mine.

3. Tom went home feeling very angry. He now wanted Pete's present.

Why did Tom behave this way?

Tom decided that Pete's game was better than his own. Tom's jealousy stopped him from enjoying his own game. It made Tom say unkind things to his parents.

If Tom had played with his own game and asked Pete if he would like to play with it too, Pete may have let Tom have a turn with his game.

1. Tom and Emma were both given new toys. Tom wanted to play with Emma's present.

2. Emma agreed and let Tom play with her car-racing set.

3. As soon as Tom saw that Emma was happy with his skateboard, he wanted it back.

Why does Tom always want what Emma has?

Tom is jealous that Emma can play happily with whatever she has. Even if Tom had the best game or toy in the world, he would still want to play with what Emma had. If Tom stopped feeling jealous about what Emma was doing, he would be able to have fun with his toys, too.

▽ *Why Can't I Have?*

Some people have more than others. This may feel unfair. You may sometimes want what someone else has. Try not to let this make you mean toward a person or make you say hurtful things. That won't change the situation.

I bet her sand is better than mine.

◁ *Same But Different*

Feeling jealous can make you believe what someone else has is always better than what you have, even if it is exactly the same!

Why not try to enjoy those things you do have instead of feeling jealous of other people's belongings. Do you still feel as jealous?

Matt, do you ever feel jealous?

"Sometimes I wish I had some of the things my friends have. But usually they let me play with their toys. There's no point in feeling jealous — you forget what good things you do have."

Why can't we have a house and garden like hers?

Jealous About People

During recess at school, Prem is telling his best friend, Adam, that he doesn't like Matt. Matt recently joined the school. Prem is jealous because Matt is now friends with Adam, as well. Oona doesn't understand why all three of them can't be friends. Have you ever felt jealous in this way?

But he's my friend.

I wish Matt had gone to another school.

Why? I think he's really friendly.

Jealousy can be about sharing friends.

It can be about a person's looks.

▽ Friends

If you are best friends with someone and he or she becomes friends with someone else you may feel jealous and no longer special. Best friends are great, but you can have other types of friends as well. The best kinds of friends are the friends you can share.

◁ Parents

If you live with one parent, it can be difficult to get used to that parent having a new partner or a special friend. But just because your mom or dad spends some time with a new partner, doesn't mean that he or she doesn't still love you.

It's not fair. She's my best friend.

▷ Brothers and Sisters

It can make you feel jealous if you think that your parents pay more attention to a brother or sister.

Each person in a family is different. Sometimes one child will need lots of attention. At other times, you may get more attention. Talk to your parents about how you feel.

Why does she always get the attention?

1. Jane didn't like Neeta. Neeta always did well at school and was picked as team captain.

2. Neeta asked Jane if she wanted to be on her team.

Why would I want to be on your team?

3. Jane was rude to Neeta and said she wouldn't be on her team.

Why was Jane rude to Neeta?

Jane was jealous that Neeta did well at school and had lots of friends. But by being rude to Neeta, Jane lost out on the chance to be on the team and to get to know Neeta and her friends. Jane's classmates thought she was very rude, so her jealousy made things even more difficult.

▼ Everyone Is Different

That's what makes the world interesting. Not everyone is good at everything. But if you try your best at whatever you are doing, then there is no reason to feel jealous.

Try to remember that what you do is just as important as what someone else is doing.

I wish I could be like them.

◀ Feeling Left Out

If you feel shy, you may be jealous of someone else who has lots of friends. But feeling jealous won't make it easier to make friends — it can make it more difficult!

Everyone can feel left out sometimes. If you see someone who looks a bit lonely, why not make a special effort to be nice to them?

Oona, do you get jealous of people?

"I used to be jealous of a girl in my school who was good at everything. It made me feel like I was hopeless. But when I talked to my mom she helped me understand that I was good at lots of things, too. After that I became friends with the other girl."

13

Jealousy Can Make You...

Last week Prem refused to go to Adam's birthday party. Adam was really upset. He couldn't understand why Prem was being unfriendly. Now Prem realizes he was unfair. He is explaining to Adam that he felt jealous. Feeling jealous can make you upset the people you love.

You may feel very angry.

You may miss out on good things.

▽ Sad Feelings

Jealousy can make you feel lots of different things. It can make you angry or lonely. It can make you forget what is good. It is hard to be happy if you spend too much time worrying about what other people do or have.

I could tear up her picture...

◁ Spoilsport

Sometimes you may feel so jealous that you want to spoil what someone else has. But ruining someone else's things won't make you feel better. It could even get you into serious trouble. Tell a grown-up about how you feel.

I hate Amy because her mom always gives her special treats.

But last week you told me about a treat your mom gave you!

... or I could tell dad how I feel.

▷ No Fun To Be With

Jealousy can make you feel mean and unkind. This can make it difficult to be friendly. It can make it hard for other people to be friends with you.

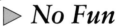

15

1. Ben was jealous of his younger brother, Tom, who always did well at school.

2. Ben deliberately broke a china ornament. He told his dad that Tom had done it.

3. Tom denied it. Their dad was angry with both of them.

Why did Ben want to get Tom into trouble?

Ben was jealous of Tom. He wanted their dad to stop thinking that Tom was so good. But getting Tom into trouble didn't make Ben's jealousy go away. It would have been better if Ben had talked to his dad about his feelings, even if his dad disagreed with him.

▼ *Feeling Cross*

Feeling jealous will only make you feel unhappy with everything you have. It can make you dislike your own toys. It can make you angry with the people you love.

> I hate all my toys.

◀ *Try Talking*

If you feel that someone else gets more attention than you, try talking to a grown-up you trust. The grown-up may not agree with your point of view and the situation may not change, but talking can help the way you feel.

Prem, are you still feeling jealous?

"A little, but I know it's not fair, and being jealous nearly lost me my best friend. I upset Adam and I was unfair to Matt, too. Matt's OK really. Now, the three of us play together."

When Someone Is Jealous Of You

After playing ball, Oona is asking Matt about school. Matt says he's enjoying it now, but he was unhappy at first because Prem was so unfriendly. Oona says she was upset when Abi was jealous of her. Talking to her mom made Oona realize she hadn't done anything wrong. It can be really upsetting when someone is jealous of you.

You may feel confused.

You may feel upset.

▽ Be Friendly

People who are jealous will also be feeling unhappy. Make them feel a bit special. Ask if they want to play with you or with your toys. It is unkind and unfair to show off or brag about what you have.

◁ Speak Up

Sometimes a person may feel so jealous that he or she will do mean things. If someone is bullying you, such as saying nasty things, hitting you, or taking things from you, tell a grown-up you trust, such as your mom, dad, or teacher.

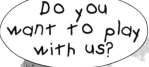

Do you want to play with us?

Matt, how did you feel when Prem was jealous of you?

"At first, I thought I had done something to upset Prem. I felt upset, too, because I thought I shouldn't be friends with Adam. Talking to someone made me feel better."

How Can You Stop Feeling Jealous?

Prem stopped feeling jealous when he realized that he was being unfair, and that Adam wouldn't want to be his friend any more. Adam says that talking to his dad helped him to stop feeling so jealous of his brother.

It can be good to share…

… and it can be good to be on your own.

▽ *Put It On Paper*

A feeling of jealousy can pass very quickly. If it doesn't, try talking to a grown-up or an older brother or sister. Sometimes it helps to get rid of the feeling by drawing a picture or writing down how you feel.

◁ *Everyone's Special*

Remember that the world is made up of lots of different people. Everyone is special and everyone is different. We all have different belongings. We all have things we are good at, and we all have things we are not so good at.

Adam, do you still feel jealous of your brother?

"If I feel jealous about something my brother Sam has done, I write down how I feel instead of getting angry with him. It helps make the feelings go away. It's much nicer when you don't feel jealous."

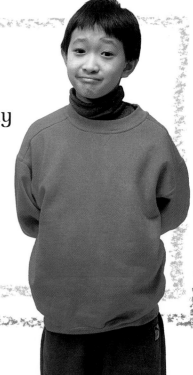

21

Don't Forget...

Matt, how do you feel now you are all friends?

"It's great. Sometimes, we go around together and sometimes we don't. Friends are brilliant, but it's good to be on your own, too."

Adam, what do you think about jealousy?

"Jealousy makes everyone feel horrible. It's always worth trying to sort it out — otherwise everyone gets hurt."

Prem, how do you feel now?

"I'm really sorry I upset my friends. I was scared that Adam preferred Matt to me. But I know now that you can like different people at the same time."

22

Oona, what can you do if someone is jealous of you?

"Try not to let it upset you. If the person is spoiling your things or saying mean things to you, tell your parents or a teacher. If you do have more things than someone else, don't show off — that's really unfair."

Abi, what can you do to stop feeling jealous?

"Talk about your feelings — being jealous is no fun. Remember the things that you do have and enjoy them. And remember that friends are more important than anything else."

23

Index

All the photographs in this book have been posed by models. The publishers would like to thank them all.